Something to Crow About!
A Bird's Tale

Suzanne Knoebel

DRAWINGS BY GIB FOSTER

GUILD PRESS OF INDIANA, INC.
Carmel, Indiana

Library of Congress
Catalog Card Number
98-72693

ISBN 1-57860-059-6

Manufactured in the United States of America.

Cover art by Gib Foster
Text design by Sheila Samson

Dedication

To all who love and seek to understand and
protect their Earth's wild cohabitants . . .

and who, by their unselfish acts,
receive love in return.

Chapter 1

BRIGHT SUNLIGHT POURED THROUGH THE LARGE PICTURE WINDOWS AS SUZIE WENT into the sunroom to change her parakeet's water and clean his cage. The cheerful rays, as they filtered through the sun catchers, cast jewel tones on the tile floor. In fact, the whole world seemed like a blaze of fresh color. Just outside the window, the lilac bush was beginning to bud, and tulip leaves were nudging their spikes up through the newly warmed ground, searching for the sun's warmth. Suzie felt a wave of spring fever wash over her. She felt like dancing. The dreary gray days of winter were over.

As she cleaned the parakeet's cage something outside caught her eye. She paused, looking at the empty lot between her house and the neighbor's. She was sure she had seen something there, but maybe she was just imagining it. No, wait — there it was again. She looked more closely, and saw a large crow walking about in a zigzag fashion, his wings spread wide.

Suzie smiled as she watched the bird, thinking that the crow was just strutting his stuff. "Just showing off," she said to herself. The bird was apparently trying to attract attention, probably to claim territory and get a mate. She had seen a television program that showed how birds would do that, particularly in the early spring. But then again, maybe he just had spring fever, too, and felt like dancing, as she did.

But when the crow turned, Suzie saw that he held his right wing tight against his body. Only the left wing was spread, its tip leaving a mark as it trailed through the early spring grass. Although the bird was holding his head high, his feathers shiny black and unruffled, it was clear that all was not well with the big crow. Suzie was almost certain he had a broken wing. She felt sorry for him.

Suzie talked to her parakeet as she cleaned his cage.

"I could feed him, but that really isn't his problem. There are lots of bugs and worms this time of year in the field and he can still walk around pretty well."

The little parakeet cocked his head and blinked his eyes as she talked, as if he understood and was thinking the same thing.

"Hmm," she said as she set the dish of fresh water in the bird cage. "I could try to catch him and keep him in the garage so he will be safe. But I don't think he would want that kind of life." She chewed her lip thoughtfully. "Well, whatever I do, I really think he needs help."

Her mother, listening at the doorway, interrupted Suzie's thoughts. "It's getting late, Suzie. You'd better get moving or you'll miss the school bus."

Suzie grabbed her books, waved good-bye to the parakeet and ran out the door. She would talk to her mother about the crow later — if he was still around, that is. Her mother might have some good ideas. She was a bird fan, too. Suzie came by it naturally. Her father sometimes joked that their house looked like a bird sanctuary, what with all the pictures and figurines of bluebirds and hummingbirds — virtually every kind of bird — and bird books on the coffee table and field guides by the windows so they could identify the birds that came to the many bird feeders they had outside all around the house. Some families loved cats and had their houses full of cat things. Suzie's family loved birds.

Among all the birds who knew the big crow, he was known as Mr. Leader because he was the chief of his family. Crow families can be quite large and Mr. Leader's was one of the largest. He and his family lived just outside the central city in a rolling area with many trees near White River called Crows Nest, testimony to the fact that the crows had lived there in large numbers before the builders had come.

Mr. Leader (alias Broken Wing — the name Suzie gave him) usually was very proud and independent. But he knew he was in trouble now. He had survived many fights and accidents before, but late in the previous afternoon he had gotten clipped by a rapidly moving car, the speed of which he hadn't quite timed accurately while he investigated some garbage on the road, looking for a delectable snack.

For Broken Wing, the first night after his accident was the worst of his life. His wing ached, and everything seemed to be more threatening than during the day. Sounds and shadows that he had never noticed before now seemed terrifying.

"I knew the owl wouldn't hurt me," he later confessed to Little Brother, the crow who was second in command after him. "But that hooting sounded so evil. I never noticed it before!"

What he didn't confess was that he talked himself into believing that the dogs he heard barking in the distance were much closer. One Dalmatian passing nearby did see him and barked furiously, but fortunately, he was on a leash and his owner kept a firm hold as he strained to go investigate Broken Wing.

Broken Wing eventually did go to sleep that first night but that was after he had found a pile of limbs that the landscape people had trimmed and piled up to be carried away when the spring clean-up was done. It was shaped so that he could hop his way up to the top and get inside a little hollow in the pile. It wasn't much protection but he felt better being a little sheltered and higher off the ground.

Early the next morning he saw his family gathering around. He was glad to see them but he stretched and acted as though he had just waked from a long peaceful rest. The younger members of the family were impressed with how brave he was, for by now all of them knew that their leader had a broken wing. Some of the older ones knew he was only putting on an act but they didn't tell the others because they admired him, too.

"We've come to watch over you until you're better," Little Brother said.

Broken Wing nodded in appreciation. "Thanks for your help. It's great to have such a fine family."

Broken Wing was much more concerned about the situation than he let on, though. When Little Brother was the only one around he discussed it with him in greater detail.

"I can't believe I let my appetite get in the way of my better judgment," he said miserably. "How stupid and careless can you be? Now I can't fly. Every cat, dog, uncaring human, and other assorted enemies will be after me. To be able to fly has always meant freedom, independence and safety for all of us. This has to be the most difficult problem I've ever faced."

Little Brother decided it would be best to get some input from the whole family.

"There has to be an answer, brother. I'll call a family meeting at Holliday Park." All the important family discussions were held at this favorite spot on the Northside of Indianapolis, and this problem definitely rated high on the importance list. Maybe one of the clan would have an idea.

৯৯

Suzie's mother, Ellen, looked out the window at the two crows, Broken Wing and Little Brother, sitting on the brush pile. Suzie had hurriedly told her about the injured bird before she went to school, and asked her mother to keep an eye on the bird, in case some predator came around.

As she watched, Ellen saw the other crows swoop down to land beside Little Brother and Broken Wing. It seemed that the crows were talking. Certainly they were making enough noise with their cawing back and forth.

She then saw the flock lift off, like a 747 jet, with Little Brother in the lead. They headed toward the Roman-looking statuary at Holliday Park, a block or so down the street.

Suzie's mother also talked to the parakeet. "Suzie is right," Ellen remarked to the little creature. "This poor bird needs help, more than the other crows can give. I guess I'll join in the bird-aid society too." The little blue parakeet winked and chirped approvingly.

&

An hour or so later, Broken Wing's clan returned to the brush pile in the empty lot. They were sad because they hadn't come up with any really good ideas.

"We did all agree that we will stay nearby and protect you as much as possible until you can fly again," Little Brother told him, and the other crows cawed their agreement. "But that still leaves you on your own at night." He spread his wings in a helpless gesture.

Broken Wing responded by making light of the subject.

"Only birds like those stupid owls can stay up all night," he shrugged. "They sleep all day. Don't worry, I'll be all right." His family had no choice. But they would stay with him as long as they could.

&

When Suzie got home from school, she dropped her backpack by the door and headed for the sunroom to look for Broken Wing. At first she didn't see him and she was glad. She thought maybe she had been wrong and that he didn't have a broken wing after all. But then she saw some crows gathered around the little brush pile where Broken Wing had spent the night. Broken Wing was sitting on top, blending with the darkness of the branches. He was flapping his good wing trying to get back to the ground. He seemed to be having more trouble moving than he had that morning.

"The time has come," Suzie said to herself as she watched him struggle. "I have to do something to help him." Suddenly she remembered that the man from the Humane Society, who had given a talk at school just a few weeks before, had told them just to call 1-800-I-HUMANE if they ever wanted to help an animal in distress. She remembered the number because it was so funny — an abbreviation for "I am humane." He hadn't mentioned birds, but surely it included them as well.

Suzie went to the kitchen where her mother was starting dinner and told her about the Humane Society man's visit.

"Why don't you give them a call?" Ellen said, smiling. "We'll know more about the possibilities after we talk to them."

As she dialed the number, Suzie wondered whether she was doing the right thing. After all, the Humane Society put dogs and cats to sleep if they couldn't be adopted. Why wouldn't they do the same with birds? She hung up and sat down, chin in hand, to think the problem through again. No matter how she turned it around, though, it always came out the same way. Broken Wing couldn't survive much longer. He needed to eat, and even if he got off the brush pile he wouldn't be able to get away from dogs and cats and other predators, particularly at night when his family couldn't be there to protect him. She'd have to call the Humane Society after all. Her mother agreed.

Although the man who answered the phone at the Injured Animal Branch of the Humane Society was very nice, after she told him the whole story he said there really wasn't anything they could do.

"We don't have anyone here who knows how to take care of birds," he sympathized. "He would probably be better off if we just put him to sleep so he won't suffer any longer."

"Oh, no. There *has* to be another way!" Suzie exclaimed. "He's a very special crow. He's so big and beautiful and I'm sure that he'll fight to live. He seems to be a leader. All of the other crows are protecting him."

The man at the other end didn't say anything for a few seconds, then said, "You might be right. Another possibility is the zoo. They have a veterinarian there who treats the zoo birds. I know her. Her name is Dr. Erica Williams. I'll call her and get back to you."

While she waited for the return call, Suzie watched Broken Wing and his family. They seemed almost frantic in the struggle with their problem. Two or three crows were always walking on the ground close to him and others swooped over him from time to time. He seemed tired. He didn't move much. That morning he had been hopping around with great energy, flapping his good wing and trying to fly. Of course, being on top of the brush pile made it difficult to be too active.

When the phone rang, Suzie ran to pick it up. "Hello," a friendly voice said. "This is Dr. Erica Williams from the zoo. I specialize in bird veterinary medicine. I hear you have an injured crow; tell me about him."

Suzie told her the story, and Dr. Williams was encouraging.

"Do you think we can catch him? If we can, I'm sure he can be helped. Most wings heal well if the bird is otherwise healthy. Crows are so smart that they are particularly good patients and can be rehabilitated quite easily."

"I'm sure we can catch him," Suzie answered eagerly. "He's on the top of a little brush pile and can't get off. If you bring a net, I'll help you."

"Good. There's still quite a bit of daylight time left. I'll be out as soon as I can and we'll see what can be done."

When she hung up the telephone, Suzie went to the window. She wanted to keep her eye on Broken Wing almost constantly. She didn't want anything to happen to him now that help was on the way.

When Dr. Williams arrived, Suzie was surprised at how young she was. The doctor in turn was also amazed that Suzie was so young. She smiled and introduced herself.

"I'm Dr. Erica Williams, but please call me Erica. Thanks for calling, Suzie. Most people, even adults, aren't concerned enough or don't take the time to care about injured animals."

Suzie shook the doctor's outstretched hand. "Well, I can't explain it, but he is so proud and has so many friends that he is difficult to ignore. He is so sure of himself that he must be quite a leader." She laughed, "He even has me working for him."

Suzie led the way toward the brush pile, and as they walked, passing budding lilacs and pussy willows that made the day seem less harsh, Erica explained her plans for Broken Wing.

"I'll take him to the zoo hospital, set the bone in proper position with some bone pins and immobilize it so that it will heal properly. I may even try some new DNA injections to stimulate healing. During the healing time we'll let him walk around the zoo."

"But won't he get awfully spoiled?" Suzie asked. "Maybe he won't want to come back to Crows Nest."

"We don't do this with most wild things because they become too accustomed to being cared for with no effort on their part and they can't be sent back to live as they had before because they'll starve," Erica agreed. "Crows, on the other hand, like people all right and get adjusted to being with them but never lose their independence. I guess they're too ornery!" she chuckled. "Don't worry. After his wing is healed, he'll be just as capable of being with his family as he ever was."

Surprisingly, Broken Wing didn't seem too afraid of Suzie and Dr. Williams as they approached with the net. He cawed out a couple of times but didn't try to get away. He seemed to sense that they only wanted to help him. His family, however, was quite upset and various members swooped down close to the two humans trying to scare them away.

"It's okay," Broken Wing cawed to his family. "I don't know how I know, but I think they're only trying to help."

Erica spoke soothingly, just as if the frantic birds could understand. "Don't worry, we'll take good care of him." Broken Wing apparently understood, for he patiently waited to be picked up and didn't try to get away. They didn't even need the net.

When Erica saw him up close she nodded and said, "You're right, Suzie, he *is* a beautiful bird, and looks very healthy. He should do very well. I'll let you know. You'll probably want to visit him." She put him in a large cage in the back of the zoo panel truck she was driving.

Suzie wasn't quite sure they should be so positive and optimistic at this stage, but she waved an enthusiastic good-bye to Broken Wing and the doctor as they drove off. As the truck turned the corner, Suzie watched for a few seconds, then went back into the house. She asked her mother if she would take her to see Broken Wing when school was out the next day, and was happy when her mother readily agreed.

Chapter 2

As soon as they got to the zoo infirmary, Dr. Williams gave Broken Wing some medicine to put him to sleep for a short while, took an x-ray of the wing, and gently moved the broken bone back into proper position. She then put a splint on the bone and fixed it with a pin at both ends. Next she wrapped an Ace bandage around his body so that both wings were immobilized.

"We have to be sure to keep both wings from moving until your broken one is all healed," she murmured softly, talking as much to herself as the groggy bird as she held him in her lap and stroked his glossy feathers. "Nature arranged wings to be stimulated in unison for coordinated flying and any attempt to move the right wing would stimulate the left and even a little motion isn't good. It slows healing."

Lying in the doctor's lap, Broken Wing enjoyed the gentle stroking of his head and neck. When she saw he was listening she said gently, "Okay, fellow, the first thing you're going to have to learn to do is walk in your new girdle. You'll think you can't for a while but you'll learn how."

She set him on the floor and he felt pretty stupid. "How in the world am I supposed to move?" he wondered. The doctor went about five feet ahead of him and held out her hand. Broken Wing saw that there was some hamburger in her palm and his hesitancy disappeared.

"I'm hungry," he said to himself. "I haven't eaten in more than a day — since my accident — and there certainly wasn't anything on the top of that dumb brush pile to eat." So he timidly moved one foot forward and then the other and found out that he didn't topple over, as he had been afraid he would. He stretched his neck out to reach the hamburger in slow-motion fashion, and then nipped hungrily at it with his beak.

The doctor laughed. "You are a brave bird. From now on, you're on your own. There is plenty of food and water in the aviary; you'll be kept safe there and you'll get your exercise looking for your food. I don't think you want to stay in the hospital overnight." She picked him up and carried him over to the aviary and gently set him inside.

"See, there is even a little trap door in the main door," Dr. Williams said. "You can go in and out as you wish. We don't want you to feel claustrophobic."

"This doesn't look too bad at all," Broken Wing said to himself as his sparkling eyes examined his surroundings. "I don't think I'll feel too penned up here."

Dr. Williams then left him there, planning to check on him every hour or so to make sure he was learning how to get along.

🎩

After the doctor left, Broken Wing just sat for a while watching passing workmen and the changing sun rays. So much had happened to him in the past several hours and he needed time to sort everything out. Besides, it was almost time to go to sleep and he really was tired.

His first thoughts were about his family. "I wonder how Little Brother is running the clan." Even though he had left his brother in charge, he had expected to stay around to offer advice whenever required. "But now," he told himself, "I have to accept that there is nothing I can do if my brother makes some bad choices. I'll have to trust that the clan will get along okay."

Broken Wing finally accepted that conclusion, deciding that he probably wouldn't be too much help anyway. "Besides," he thought, "when you have problems as big as mine, it's hard to keep being a leader. Good leadership depends on thinking about what others need rather than what you need." And he was a good leader. He had spent his adult years thinking first of what was best for the family, not just himself.

He resigned himself to the situation. "I don't really know where I am anyway. I couldn't tell which direction I was going in that zoo truck. I don't think I'm very far away — as the crow flies," he said, allowing himself a bit of wry humor. But, as with the first problem, he couldn't do anything about finding out where he was right now anyway. "That will have to wait until I can fly again."

Broken Wing realized that most importantly, he needed to concentrate on getting well. Everything else could be solved after that. So, because he was still hungry, he went in search of more food and water and then a place to sleep.

When morning came, Broken Wing nudged the little door that the doctor had showed him open with his head and walked through it with some difficulty — for he really hadn't learned to balance himself completely as yet in his girdle. He found himself outside in a giant wire pen about twenty feet long and ten feet high, with a top made of the same kind of fencing as the sides. The enclosure was full of sunshine and fresh air, so he didn't feel trapped. Looking around, he realized the pen was for him. "If there weren't a top," he reasoned, "other and perhaps less friendly crows might come down and eat my food and peck at me." He decided it would be all right to stay in this place until his wing healed. He thought of the brush pile and the scary night noises and shadows, and let out a crow sigh. "It could be worse by a whole lot." He was a bit lonely, however, despite the fact that he could see other animals and birds in pens farther away. He didn't know how to talk to them though.

The doctor, looking out of her office window that overlooked the pens, was glad to see that Broken Wing was already up and exploring. It was a good sign. As she had promised, she called Suzie. When Suzie's mother answered the phone, Dr. Williams told her, "Everything is all right so far. Please tell Suzie that I'll call again soon."

"In the meantime," Dr. Williams continued, "feel free to come see him anytime during zoo hours. But don't be alarmed at his body wrap. It's just to keep the healing wing from too much motion."

Chapter 3

THE DOCTOR NEARLY ALWAYS TOOK ONE OF HER LESS SICK PATIENTS WITH HER ON rounds. As the days went by she found herself more often choosing Broken Wing as a companion. He made her laugh. When she put him down in her office or on the ground so that he could walk slowly with her around the zoo, he was always looking for bits of paper to play with, throwing them into the air and ducking so they wouldn't touch him when they floated down. Or he pecked at imaginary grains of corn. Sometimes he played hide and seek with her, hiding behind a bush or tree and acting very haughty when she'd find him.

One day Erica decided she would take him with her to the gate as she greeted a group of fifth-grade children from a nearby school who were coming to tour the zoo and to hear a lecture on ways to protect wildlife.

Of course, almost the first thing the children noticed was Broken Wing in his funny looking body wrap. They were full of questions for the doctor.

"He looks like a mummy," said Sarah, a tall, thoughtful-seeming girl wearing a too-short skirt. "What happened to him? Can he walk with that girdle on?" Some of the girls giggled when they heard that question.

One of the other girls, with her hair gathered back and flipped up and held in place by a red barrette, commented, "He must be pretty hot with that girdle on." She fanned herself with her sun hat, emphasizing the point that it was a very warm early June day. Some of the children's noses already were reddened by the late spring sun.

"Will he get well?" another asked.

"Can he talk?"

"Will he ever go home?"

The questions came fast and eagerly, all of the children talking at once.

The doctor smiled and told them the story of Broken Wing up until that very day, at least as much as she knew.

Erica pointed to a boy with a missing front tooth and a hand waving eagerly in the air. "My name is George," he said. "What do you think will happen with Broken Wing once he can fly again and is given the choice of whether to stay at the zoo or go home?"

Dr. Williams wanted to test the children's imaginations. "What do the rest of you think?"

There were almost as many guesses as to what he would or should do after his wing healed as there were members of the class. The kids were raising their hands to be picked to give their opinion.

"He'll stay here where life is pretty soft. After all, he doesn't have to worry about anything, does he?" George said.

The boy next to George wasn't quite so sure that was a good decision, saying, "But he wouldn't have any close friends that understand him unless the zoo gets some more crows."

Sarah said, "Well, I think Broken Wing will probably go home and live happily ever after." One of her friends laughed and said, "You've been reading too many fairy tales. Life, even for crows, isn't that simple."

Steve, a serious-minded business executive-type of boy dressed in a crisp white shirt and neatly pressed khaki slacks, said, "He may go home but he may find that things have changed. Maybe the other crows won't recognize him or even want him around, and he'll be an outsider. In that case, he should stay here at the zoo." Steve was a practical person, and didn't want Broken Wing to take any risks.

The young veterinarian considered all of the students' thoughts when the discussion quieted down after a while. "We're going to have to wait and see," she concluded. "We don't know what Broken Wing is thinking. He seems pretty happy here but maybe he's just making the best of a bad deal."

After a few more seconds, she continued, "I'll be sure to let you know what happens. I'll write a letter to you all at school. Now let's go and see the dolphins and the penguins."

The group of fifth graders, their teacher, Dr. Williams, and Broken Wing all started up the path toward the dolphin building. Dr. Williams stooped down and picked Broken Wing up. "You probably wouldn't be able to keep up with this fast-moving group, as eager as they are to see everything," she told him. But Broken Wing had other ideas and struggled to be let down until Dr. Williams gave up and let him join the kids. The groundskeeper was planting petunias along the walkway to welcome the summer, and the class crowded around to watch for a moment.

About that time Suzie's mother dropped her off, and Suzie joined the tour group. She walked beside Broken Wing, talking to him as they went. If birds could smile, he would have. He walked alongside Suzie, holding his head high and hoping she liked him as much as he did her.

Chapter 4

THE ZOO PARKING LOT WAS NEARLY FULL. SCHOOL WAS OUT FOR THE SUMMER AND children, babies in strollers, and doting grandparents crowded the pathways of the zoo. But, most importantly, this was the day when Dr. Williams proclaimed that Broken Wing's bone was healed. She had invited Suzie and her mother for Broken Wing's reentry into normal crow life. "The x-ray shows that a firm seal had been formed, joining the ends of the bone at the place where the break occurred," she told them.

Dr. Williams took Broken Wing's body wrap off, speaking soothingly to him as she worked. "We really should give you a new name," she said. "But since we all know you by 'Broken Wing,' I guess you're going to be stuck with that one."

She set him down on the hospital floor, and once again, he wasn't sure he could walk, let alone fly. He had to learn to balance himself all over again. He blinked and didn't move right away, obviously unsure of himself. Erica laughed and said, "You'll do it, big boy. You did it before when we wrapped you up like a mummy and you'll soon get your flight wings again." She motioned to Suzie and her mother, "Let's leave him alone while he experiments."

So the rehabilitation process at the zoo began. After a few days, Broken Wing would hop up on a box or a tree stump and then do a combination hop-fly. Wanting to impress Suzie, he picked a day when she was visiting to show off. Unfortunately, he found that he wasn't quite as rehabilitated as he thought and had lost some strength and fell with a thud rather than making a graceful two-point landing on a box. "So, I'm out of shape," he told himself making light of his awkwardness. Suzie laughed and gave him some corn to eat. "That was funny but don't do it again!" she said.

Gradually, however, his strength returned and he was able to fly to the top of some smaller trees and around the zoo. He realized it was time for some decision-making about his future. The doctor thought so, too, and she and Suzie discussed their plans.

Erica told Suzie, "Broken Wing doesn't know that the band that was placed on his leg when I brought him to the zoo also contains a radio transmitting and receiving device. I have tried to train him like they do homing pigeons. During his time at the zoo I have been conditioning him to respond to a radio signal sent out from my office."

If only she had known that Broken Wing often wondered about the sensations from the band caused by the radio transmissions. "What is that tingling in my leg?" he asked himself. "Oh, well, maybe it's just part of getting better." He trusted his human friends completely by now.

The doctor had decided to band the crow after reading about a study the Army had done with carrier pigeons. She wanted to try it for Broken Wing because she didn't want him to get lost if he wanted to come back to the zoo after he was released. The radio range for the band was just a little beyond Crows Nest and she could send out intermittent transmissions to the band device so that Broken Wing could have a signal to follow back to the zoo. "If after a while he becomes well adjusted in his family circle again, we'll stop sending signals," she told Suzie. "In the meantime, he can try out both living spots."

Dr. Williams called Suzie the next day. "I think the best way to start the decision process is to take Broken Wing home for a short visit and see how well he does. When will you be at home so we can both watch out for him?"

Suzie replied, "Tomorrow will be fine with me if it is convenient for you."

They agreed to meet at about seven in the morning. Dr. Williams guessed, "The crows will be finished with their breakfast by that time and will be ready to greet Broken Wing."

The next morning, Suzie and Erica took Broken Wing to the lot where they had found him after he had been injured. The brush pile was gone by now, but Erica set him down at that spot and she and Suzie walked away, standing near the house to watch what he would do.

Broken Wing sat very quietly for a while, feeling a bit uncertain. "Now what am I supposed to be doing?" he wondered. Finally, however, he stretched high on his toes, flapped his wings, strutted, and gave out several very commanding caws.

The response was almost immediate. At least a dozen crows appeared from the nearby woods, circled around, and landed next to him. They seemed to be excited and friendly. After a short while these crows left and others arrived. There was almost a continuous stream of visitors. Broken Wing greeted them all royally.

Suzie smiled and said, "It looks as though they haven't forgotten him. I wonder what they're talking about."

"We'll have to guess depending on what he decides to do — stay or come back to the zoo with me," Erica responded. "Let's give him a bit more time then I'll go see if he wants me to pick him up."

After about an hour of the reunion, Dr. Williams walked over to the vacant lot and knelt down. Broken Wing walked into her outstretched hands.

Suzie joined them and she and the doctor talked some more. "It looks as if he's ready to go back to the zoo, unless he wants you to live here with him," Suzie said laughingly.

Dr. Williams stroked Broken Wing's head and said, "We'll try this over and over again until we're sure he's made up his mind. I may leave him here for a day or so occasionally and then turn on the transmitter so he'll know how to get back and forth if that's what he wants to do. In the meantime, it's back to the zoo for today."

She stood up, with Broken Wing in her arms, and said, "Suzie, I think we have something really good going here. We'll be back."

Broken Wing was glad to hear that he would be back. He hadn't quite decided yet where he wanted to live.

Chapter 5

WHAT BROKEN WING HAD LEARNED DURING HIS VISIT HOME WAS THAT HIS FAMILY had gotten along very well while he was gone. While they were all glad to see him, none suggested that they needed him in a leadership role. In fact, all the crows seemed to be looking toward Little Brother.

"It seems the family likes your being the leader," Broken Wing said to Little Brother. "How do you like it?"

His brother replied, "It's great — I never knew you had so much fun! We take trips to the corn fields just west of Springmill Road up north. Sometimes we follow White River as it winds downtown. And sometimes we just tease rabbits and chipmunks — they think we're hawks."

Broken Wing couldn't resist a retort. "You haven't hit the rough spots yet, I guess." He recognized a little jealousy nagging at him so he said, "I'm happy all's going well." And he was.

But still he would have liked to solve just one little problem. He needed to feel needed.

One of his oldest friends, Mame, an old aunt crow with a chipped beak, settled next to him to preen her feathers and talk for a while.

"I'm sorry you've had so much trouble, with your wing and all," she sympathized. Broken Wing didn't feel like talking about it, so he cut the conversation short by saying, "It isn't any fun but the world keeps going on and we will, too. At least I've learned you need to keep being useful or you'll wind up being isolated and unhappy."

As the weeks went by, Broken Wing had the opportunity to talk with many family members. There was Strutting Big John, Timid Joe, Cousin Sam and Hildy, his girlfriend, among others. Sometimes they came to meet him at the zoo now that they knew where he was. They flapped their wings to let him know they were there and he would join them as they flew straight — as the crow flies — to home base, Crows Nest. Sometimes he flew to Holliday Park so he could chat with them there. His personal route to Crows Nest followed White River. The route was greener and less congested, and he could fly over the beautiful, tree-lined river itself. There was no traffic there, except for an occasional fishing boat, and no exhaust fumes. While the route took him farther west than he

needed to go, he enjoyed the sights (even though he didn't know their names) — Butler University and Crown Hill Cemetery, with its little stone "houses" topping the bump of a hill. He would often stop for a while at the Indianapolis Museum of Art; with all of the outdoor sculptures, its fountain, and the breathtaking view of the river, it was one of his favorite resting spots. Then further south was the Veterans Hospital, Indiana University Medical Center, the track and field stadium, and even a new park where men threw balls at other men who would swing clubs to knock the balls away. Broken Wing found the things humans enjoyed puzzling at times. Sometimes when he was in a hurry to get back to the zoo he would cut off the west loop of White River, dropping down to Fall Creek then over to White River again. The river was his anchor.

One day as the clan relaxed after a meeting at Holliday Park, Broken Wing said to Cousin Sam, "There are benefits to being out of the leadership business. For example, you can be close to your friends without looking like you're playing favorites."

"None of the family ever felt like you had favorites," Sam replied. "Besides, you've always brought happiness wherever you are. You always tell us how great we are even when we aren't. You make us laugh by making human sounds at times — like when you say, 'Fido, here Fido!' like that lady next to Crows Nest does when she calls her dog."

Although Sam's words made Broken Wing feel better, he discovered that he more frequently was glad when it was time to go to the zoo and make rounds with Dr. Williams. While he occasionally missed the freedom he'd had as just an ordinary crow, the

feeling of satisfaction that came with doing things for the zoo and its visitors, even if it was just making them proud and happy, was worth keeping up with the strict rules of the doctor's schedule.

Still, he found himself venturing farther from the zoo grounds more often. One day he would go to the museum next to the zoo and look at the Indian statues, or he would fly west all the way to the airport. He never went so far that he didn't feel comfortable about finding his way back. A couple of times when he got a little nervous about getting back to the zoo he felt a tingle from the band around his leg and there seemed to be something that pointed him in the right direction.

On one particular fall day, during one of his excursions straight west of town, he saw a flock of strange crows in a newly harvested cornfield snacking on the leftover ears and kernels. Broken Wing decided he could stand a bite to eat and a little conversation. He landed and cautiously walked around for a few minutes, and decided the group was friendly. He moved close to one of the younger-looking crows and asked, "Which crow is your leader?"

"Come on, I'll show you," the young crow said, and took him over to a large bird whose black-blue coat glistened in the autumn sunlight. Broken Wing, although no slouch himself, felt a twinge of jealousy. He introduced himself simply as "Mr. Wing" instead of Broken Wing because he didn't want to get into that long story; and he wasn't a leader anymore so to introduce himself as "Mr. Leader" would have been deceptive.

"I might be a prankster, but I'm not dishonest," Broken Wing laughed to himself.

While they walked together, picking up a kernel of Indian corn here or a big grasshopper there, the other crow leader told him about his group's sad state of affairs.

"We're probably going to have to move our flock to some other area. This part of the country is just getting too dangerous." The leader sighed and shook his head sadly. "There are too many people what with all these new subdivisions, too many cars, too many boys with air rifles, and really not enough food. We've tried to talk the Crows Nest group into moving also, but they don't want to hurt their old leader's feelings or abandon him. Apparently he got hurt or something, and even though they think he's too old to be useful anymore, they feel they owe him a familiar place to come to."

Broken Wing turned away from the other crow. He didn't know whether to be sad that his family thought he was old and useless, or to be glad they thought so much of him. Nevertheless, he realized with a bit of a shock that once again he had been thinking of himself, trying to make up his mind where he wanted to live when he had a whole family tied down because of him!

Well, his mind was made up now. He walked over to the other leader crow and said, "Good-bye. I enjoyed meeting and talking with you, but I must be on my way home now." As he flew away he realized when he thought of "home" he had thought of the zoo, and that's what it would be from now on.

The very next day Broken Wing flew the White River route to Crows Nest. He ar-

rived in the lot next to Suzie's house at morning feeding time. Although the sun was still warm like summertime, there was the feel of fall in the air and the maple trees were beginning to show shades of yellow and orange.

Broken Wing went directly to Little Brother.

"I've heard some other crows saying that this area is getting dangerous. Is that right?" he asked.

"Well, we have had some trouble," Little Brother said. "Big John got shot and killed last week. And if that wasn't bad enough, the boys that shot him hung his body on that post over there. I suppose they thought it would scare us off. But mostly the problem is that we're running out of feeding space. Most of the land in Crows Next has long since built up. Now the last two lots are sold. There is space in Holliday Park but another crow family has moved in and they aren't too friendly."

"Do you think it's time to move?" Broken Wing asked.

Little Brother looked a bit uneasy. He finally nodded, "Well, it's something to consider. Actually we have been talking about it."

"I know I'm not really the leader anymore and you don't need to do as I say, but I think you ought to go," Broken Wing said, trying to make it easy. "I'll miss you all but I've got a lot to do at the zoo and I'm not going to be able to be over here much anymore." He felt a lump in his craw.

Relieved, Little Brother's enthusiasm broke through. "I think it would be great for all of us. And we wouldn't forget about you, of course. Some of us will come over to visit you from time to time."

"Sure you will, and that will be great," Broken Wing said as he turned away from his brother and tried hard to swallow the lump in his throat. "Well, ahem, I've got to make my rounds at the zoo soon. I'll see you later." He took off.

He brooded all the way back to the zoo. "Things change," he said to himself over and over. "You can't always do the same things that once made you happy. You need to fly in new directions now and then."

Besides, there *was* a lot to do at the zoo and he *did* feel useful. When he went to the front gate of the zoo to welcome visitors he always was the center of attention, and because of their interest in him the visitors learned a lot about crows. And that served not only his family but all crows. Crows had suffered a bad name for a long time. They were always the birds that farmers tried to scare away with those ugly dummy figures in the fields — scarecrows. Whenever someone had to backtrack on something they had said or done, the saying was that, "they had to eat crow." That sounded bad — and humans thought so too.

Actually, Broken Wing had always told the young birds in his family that crows are very useful and reliable world citizens. He readily admitted that they had annoying habits such as swooping down on a farmer's field and eating everything in sight. On the other hand, he always countered by pointing out their good qualities.

"We crows do a lot of good by eating lots of insects and worms that otherwise gobble up crops," he said proudly.

A story well known in crow circles told of a farmer north of Indianapolis, near Carmel, who offered a reward for dead crows. He ended up losing all of his crops because they were destroyed by grub worms that the crows would have eaten.

By the time Broken Wing got home he had it all figured out. He would stay at the zoo, greet people at the gate, make them laugh.

"And maybe I'll have a little fun myself," he said hopefully. He had to admit that it wasn't what he really wanted. He would rather live as wild crows should live — free and independent and proud. At the zoo he would have to do what humans wanted, and he knew that not all humans could be trusted. But he had his family to think about. He wanted them to feel free to move and do what was best for them without having to worry about him.

He made it clear to Dr. Williams and Suzie that he had made up his mind. He didn't fly back to Crows Nest the next day or any of the days that followed. He got his exercise flying around the city and the suburbs, north south, east, and west. He couldn't believe the spreading clusters of human homes and the large parks full of low buildings where humans worked. There was something new all the time.

Chapter 6

Dr. Williams wrote to the boys and girls in the fifth-grade class Broken Wing had greeted when he first lived at the zoo and read it to Suzie over the phone for her approval.

September 1, 1998

Dear Students:

I wanted to let you know that Broken Wing has decided to stay at the zoo. Every time I've taken him to visit his family, he stays for shorter and shorter periods and seems now not to want to have me leave him at all. When I put him on the ground, he follows me when I try to walk away. So, of course, I pick him up again and take him back to the zoo with me.

He can fly very well now. In fact, when other crows visit him, some of which might be from his family, he flies around the zoo with them but seems to be perfectly happy when they leave. After all, he is a busy bird. He is now our official visitor greeter and hardly ever misses a group tour. He also has made many friends among the other birds and animals at the zoo. He entertains them well.

Please come to visit Broken Wing and the zoo again.

Thanks for your interest.

> *Sincerely,*
> *Erica Williams, D.V.M.*
> *Indianapolis Zoo*

"That sounds fine to me," Suzie said. "I'd enjoy getting a letter like that."

"Sarah wondered whether Broken Wing would live happily ever after here at the zoo," Erica laughed. "I hope this reassures her."

A couple of weeks later Dr. Williams sent a copy of the letter to the fifth-graders to Suzie, adding a handwritten note at the bottom, thanking her again for her concern. The note said:

The zoo is now famous for its "almost-human" crow. People come from all over the country to have their shoestrings untied by Broken Wing or their pocket handkerchiefs stolen. He has gotten a little mischievous. Some say he is very spoiled. I think he's just having fun because he is contributing in a meaningful way to others' pleasure.

He says "Hello" when tour groups arrive and has his picture on pamphlets about crows that I've prepared. It points out the crows' value and the fact that the Biological Society has recommended their protection because the good they do outweighs their bad habits.

Incidentally, Suzie, I'm going to be leaving the zoo in a few days to take a research fellowship. I'll let you know where I am so we can keep in touch.

Sincerely,

Erica

Tears stung Suzie's eyes as she read the note. But they were happy tears. Happy for Broken Wing, for herself, and for all who would benefit from knowing about crows and being entertained by Broken Wing. She felt sure that he would live out his life productively at the zoo.

But it wasn't to be that simple. The story hadn't ended.

Suzie got a telephone call one afternoon just as she arrived home from school. It was from Mr. Zidell, the new zoo plant manager. She had never even heard of him.

Mr. Zidell was blunt. "I see from our records that you are listed as the responsible person for a big crow listed as Broken Wing. I'm calling to let you know that we are going to destroy him within forty-eight hours."

Suzie was stunned. "Why in the world would you do that?" She almost yelled into the phone.

"Because he's a pest!" the man snapped, not even trying to be kind. "Since Dr. Williams left he hangs around the gate all of the time, messing up the sidewalks and flower beds. And now the neighborhood boys are throwing rocks at him just to see him dodge — which he's pretty good at actually — and he's become aggressive. He flies and pecks at the little children and scares them, and I can't have a bunch of kids crying the minute they hit the entrance to the zoo. I've got him in a cage now and he has to be gotten rid of. The only reason I'm calling you is because I'm legally obligated to let you know."

"Does Dr. Williams know about this?" Suzie was frantic. She hadn't heard from Erica yet and didn't even know where she was.

"I haven't the foggiest. Besides, it wouldn't make any difference!" He hung up.

Suzie had to find Erica right away. She decided to start once again with the 1-800-I HUMANE number, but that was no help. No one seemed to know where Dr. Williams had gone. It was as though she had just disappeared. The people at the Humane Society didn't even know she had left the zoo. The last person she talked to suggested that she call the Veterinary Association to see if Dr. Williams had perhaps transferred her license and given them a forwarding address or telephone number. No help. Dr. Williams was still listed as zoo veterinarian.

The Veterinary Association suggested Suzie call the National Audubon Society to see if they had received a change of address form for Dr. Williams. She got no answer there. A recorded message said that they were closed for repairs and would open again in two weeks. Suzie sat for a moment after she hung up, chewing her lip.

Feeling that she must do something, Suzie begged her mother to take her to see Broken Wing. But as soon as she got there, she wished she hadn't come; it only made her feel worse. The fall day was chilly and damp, and there in the drizzling rain sat a dejected crow in a padlocked cage. His soggy feathers had lost their luster. His name could well be Broken Spirit now. His eyes were as dull as his feathers. The sharp bright look in them was gone. The zoo was nearly deserted now that school had started, and dry and blowing leaves rattled against his cage. Suzie knelt in front of the cage, talking to Broken Wing, but he just huddled in the far corner and stared listlessly, not even looking at her.

"Oh, Mom," she said, fighting back tears. "What can I do? I just can't let anything happen to him now!"

Suzie turned the problem over in her mind on the drive home, and an idea struck her.

"I know!" she exclaimed to her mother. "I'll call Penny!"

Penny was one of Erica's friends whom Suzie and her mother had met at a zoo lecture. She might have an idea where Dr. Williams was. But Penny wasn't home, so Suzie left a message on the answering machine.

"My name is Suzie, and I'm a friend of Dr. Williams. I need to get in touch with her about the crow at the zoo. They are going to destroy him. Please call right away." Suzie left her phone number and hung up, more worried than ever.

Unless Penny called that evening, leaving the message wouldn't do any good at all. Suzie's parents had plans to take her to Brown County to the family cabin for the long weekend of the fall break, and were leaving the next morning. Even though she didn't think it would work, she asked her mother if they could postpone the trip.

"Oh, Suzie," her mother said. "I know you're worried about the crow, but we've had this weekend planned for a long time. Uncle Bill and Aunt Marge are coming with your cousins, and we almost never get to see them. Besides," Ellen soothed, "don't forget that we do have a phone at the cabin."

The next morning as Suzie and her parents were loading up the car the phone rang. Suzie ran back to answer.

"Is this Suzie?" a woman asked. "I'm Penny's mother. Penny's out of town, and I'm taking care of her house while she's gone. I checked her answering machine this morning and thought your message sounded serious enough to call back on. Penny's on an Alaskan tour. She won't be back for another week."

Suzie looked helplessly at the calendar above the phone desk. "Is there any way to get in touch with her?"

"Well, I do have an '800' number for the lodge where she's staying part of the time."

"Oh, please, may I have it?" Suzie asked. "Time is running out for Broken Wing."

She wrote the number down and thanked Penny's mother for calling, and Suzie's parents agreed to wait long enough for her to try to reach Penny.

Deciding this was Broken Wing's last chance, Suzie said a little prayer and dialed the number for the lodge in Alaska.

"No, the party you're calling for has not checked in yet. Would you care to leave a message?"

Suzie left her name and the number where she could be reached at the cabin.

She had done her best, but it was all such a long shot. After all, as far as she knew, Penny was just a casual friend of Dr. Williams.

Suzie's mother was just coming back into the house to get her. "The car's running, Suzie. You've left your messages and there's no point waiting any longer. You're holding up Dad and me."

"But Broken Wing is getting closer to death every minute!" Suzie cried.

Her mother sighed and stroked Suzie's hair. "I'm sorry, dear. I don't mean to act like I don't care, but there's nothing more we can do right now. Maybe Mr. Zidell's call was just a first warning. You might find Dr. Williams yet. You've left enough messages around."

Chapter 7

AFTERWARD, SUZIE COULDN'T HELP BUT WONDER WHAT MADE HER DECIDE TO STAY AT the cabin when everyone else went into Nashville to dinner and a play.

She had just fallen asleep but woke up quickly when the phone rang.

"This is Penny, Dr. Williams' friend. My mother said you called and said it was important."

"You wouldn't by any chance know where Dr. Williams is, would you?" Suzie went right to the point.

"You called me in Alaska to find out where Erica Williams is?" Penny sounded like she didn't believe it. Then she laughed. "It just so happens she's right here."

Suzie couldn't believe her good fortune, and the next thing she knew, Erica was on the other end and Suzie was spilling out the whole story to her.

Erica listened, asking questions now and then. Once she had the whole story she was silent for a moment, then said firmly, "Don't worry about it any more, Suzie. I had my eye on that fellow, the new plant manager, ever since he started working at the zoo, about a month before I left. There's something that's not quite right about him, and I've been trying to get something on him for quite a while now."

"He's not the kind who should be running anything," Erica continued, "let alone a zoo where kindness and understanding of our furred and feathered friends is the goal. Zidell's job is to make sure food and supplies for the animals were ordered on time and in the right amount, and that the facilities were clean and all the other housekeeping chores kept up — but *not* to decide which bird or animal lives or dies."

Suzie gave a big sigh of relief. "So can you make sure nothing bad happens to Broken Wing, and that he isn't left out in the rain any more?" she asked.

"Not to worry," Erica said. "I'll take care of that guy when I get back. We'll also take care of Broken Wing. He's smart and we can rehabilitate him. I hope he still has his radio transmitter on."

"But this is his execution day!" Suzie was still nervous.

"Mr. Big-Shot Plant Manager had better worry about himself and not about getting rid of Broken Wing," Erica said. "I guarantee, I'll make some calls and take care of it right away. The zoo director is a good man and likes Broken Wing, too. I'm sure he has no idea what Zidell has planned. Maybe I'll sweeten the deal and even promise to come back after my fellowship is done."

Reassured, Suzie thanked Erica and they said their good-byes with promises to keep in touch. Suzie heard a car pull up to the cabin and headed out to the porch to meet her returning family. Her heart and mind were both light and gay. She trusted Dr. Williams completely.

The next zoo newsletter carried the story that a new plant manager had been hired to replace Mr. Zidell, who was moving on to "new opportunities." Suzie's mother and father were amused as the three of them talked about it over pizza and Cokes.

"Imagine, all of this upset over a crow!" her father joked. "Broken Wing must be pretty important. I guess you could say Mr. Zidell really had to 'eat crow,' right, Suzie?" He popped a piece of pepperoni in his mouth for emphasis and winked.

Suzie winced. "Dad, that's not a very nice thing to say! Broken Wing is part of the family!"

While Suzie and her parents laughed over the situation, Suzie wondered how Dr. Williams had actually accomplished getting Mr. Zidell fired.

On Saturday Suzie went to the zoo to verify Broken Wing's release from his cage.

The director met them personally and told them that the board of trustees had asked Erica to postpone her planned fellowship for a short time until they could straighten out the mess that the fired plant manager had made of things. Erica had agreed, not too unhappily, for she had missed the zoo and her move into the world of research was a little daunting. The short delay gave her a sense of relief; she could complete her research later.

The gray days and rain of November, the bare trees and absence of children's voices just added to Broken Wing's dismal mood. It was true that he had been released and was treated very well now, but even though he was back on duty he felt no joy about it. He had learned, again, that not all humans could be trusted. He had to have his independence even if it meant dying for it. He wanted to go back to Crows Nest but didn't know whether he would find his family there. He'd heard from other birds passing by that many of them had left; those who had stayed hadn't visited him lately. A sarcastic bluejay remarked that maybe the crows thought Broken Wing was dead.

Erica Williams had noticed the big crow's restlessness and lack of enthusiasm. He seemed withdrawn and spent a lot of time just standing in the patch of still-green grass that bordered a pond in the center of the zoo. He wasn't the same crow she had left. She asked Suzie to come down to the zoo so they could discuss Broken Wing's future. They met in Erica's office, out of the rain and wind, with Broken Wing invited as well. The bird was still quite leery of humans, and kept somewhat distant from Suzie and Erica.

They had decided to eat lunch at Erica's desk while they met. Broken Wing, enticed by the prospect of a handout, had been edging closer to the desk. As she reached for a potato chip, Erica suddenly felt a sharp nip on her leg.

"Ouch!" She looked down and saw Broken Wing, head cocked to one side and blinking, trying to look innocent. She motioned to Suzie to look down at the mischievous bird.

"Seems we have ignored our feathered friend about as long as he can stand it. What do you think we ought to do with him?" They spoke as if they thought Broken Wing could understand them. Little did they know that he did, and what he was trying to show them.

"I wonder if these humans understand me," Broken Wing said to himself. "Why do they think I pecked the healer's ankle? Just meanness? I just want them to understand that I know these two care about me."

Suzie offered a potato chip to Broken Wing, but to her disappointment the bird just eyed it suspiciously.

"Poor Broken Wing," she said. "You used to eat our chips without even being invited. Being punished and caged has made you not trust anyone." She sighed and said to Erica, "I suppose we could take him back to his family. Then he'd have to hunt for his food and companionship again. He'd find out how tough life can be without us."

Erica smiled. "Suzie, you really are wise beyond your years," she said. "Maybe this episode with Broken Wing has had something to do with your maturity. Thinking about others does that.

"And I think you have a good point," she continued. "Let's take him back to Crows Nest. Maybe some of his family is still there. We'll turn the transmitter on every hour or so in case he wants to come back. If he doesn't he'll learn to ignore it and we'll turn it off after a while."

The ride back to Crows Nest was full of what-ifs for Suzie, Erica, and Broken Wing. However, it didn't take long for them to see what Broken Wing had decided. As soon as they set him on the ground in the lot where he had spent most of his life, he stood high on his toes, spread his wings, and gave a raucous caw. A dozen or so crows immediately swooped down and flocked around him. They all began cawing at once. They sounded happy.

Suzie and the doctor laughed, and Erica said, "Look's like he's really got something to crow about. They haven't forgotten him. It's nice to be that important."

Broken Wing returned to the zoo only three or four times at the beckoning of the radio beam. Finally, after two weeks when she didn't see Broken Wing, Dr. Williams turned off the signaling device.

The crows didn't leave Crows Nest after all. They still frequented the empty lot by Suzie's house, and they could be seen holding their meetings at the ruins in Holliday Park. Suzie always was thrilled to see Broken Wing's family when they took flight, the large flock spread out like an ebony blanket as they mounted into the air over Crows Nest. The birds seemed comfortable and to have adjusted to being increasingly surrounded with humans. Maybe they were learning to live with change, too.

Several times over the next summer, Suzie would look out the sunroom window and see a big crow that looked very much like Broken Wing. She couldn't be certain, of course, but the crow didn't seem afraid whenever she would approach him. Even so, she didn't try to coax him to her because she had grown wiser, too. He had earned his freedom and obviously that was where his heart lay. Suzie was determined not to interfere with what was best for Broken Wing.

Besides, for Suzie, it was back to studying harder than ever. Her career goal had switched from astronaut to veterinarian.